YOUR KNOWLEDGE HAS VALUE

- We will publish your bachelor's and master's thesis, essays and papers

- Your own eBook and book - sold worldwide in all relevant shops

- Earn money with each sale

Upload your text at www.GRIN.com
and publish for free

Bibliographic information published by the German National Library:

The German National Library lists this publication in the National Bibliography; detailed bibliographic data are available on the Internet at http://dnb.dnb.de .

This book is copyright material and must not be copied, reproduced, transferred, distributed, leased, licensed or publicly performed or used in any way except as specifically permitted in writing by the publishers, as allowed under the terms and conditions under which it was purchased or as strictly permitted by applicable copyright law. Any unauthorized distribution or use of this text may be a direct infringement of the author s and publisher s rights and those responsible may be liable in law accordingly.

Imprint:

Copyright © 2019 GRIN Verlag
Print and binding: Books on Demand GmbH, Norderstedt Germany
ISBN: 9783346027283

This book at GRIN:

https://www.grin.com/document/501530

Kimberley Bartolo

The Process of the Development of the Addictive Career. Young People and Addictive Behaviour

GRIN Verlag

GRIN - Your knowledge has value

Since its foundation in 1998, GRIN has specialized in publishing academic texts by students, college teachers and other academics as e-book and printed book. The website www.grin.com is an ideal platform for presenting term papers, final papers, scientific essays, dissertations and specialist books.

Visit us on the internet:

http://www.grin.com/

http://www.facebook.com/grincom

http://www.twitter.com/grin_com

University of Malta

Faculty for Social Wellbeing

Department of Youth Studies

Young People and Addictive Behaviour

Assignment

Kimberley Bartolo

B.A. (Hons) in Social Wellbeing Studies

Discuss the process of the development of the addictive career, making reference to theoretical perspectives presented in the course.

Introduction

The term addiction is commonly alluded in the day-to-day conversations between individuals (example, I am a chocolate addict); yet, not much thought is given on what the construct actually means (McMurran, 1994; Shaffer, 2017). As a matter of fact, the word 'addiction' is quiet difficult to interpret because everyone has different meanings and connotations to it depending on the believes and knowledge that each individual has as well as, the context that it is used in (Moss & Dyer, 2010; Thombs & Osborn, 2013). In spite of this, a common understanding of the term amongst researchers is that addiction is a type of chronic disorder that transpires when an individual develops some sort of habit that is beyond his conscious control and that is persistently repeated, regardless of the negative consequences that the habit may have on the individual himself or on others (Henderson, 2000; Ross & Kincaid, 2010; West & Brown, 2013; Ryan, 2014; Bedell, 2015; Diclemente, 2018).

However, such an open understanding of the term took time to get established. Back in the days, addictive behaviours where only considered as being substance-related disorders, in fact, the Diagnostic and Statistical Manual of Mental Disorders (DSM-III-R) used to define it as being compulsive drug use, which are characterized by withdrawal symptoms (West & Brown, 2013; Potenza, 2014). Nowadays, the term has evolved and professionals understand that addiction is not just substance related. The DSM-5 extended the definition from 'Substance-related disorders' by adding '... and Addictive disorders' to the original meaning (American Psychiatric Association, 2013; Potenza, 2014; Pinna et al., 2015). The definition has transitioned and behaviours like, gambling and internet use, are now also taken into consideration as being behavioural addictions because they share various elements (Moss & Dyer, 2010; Clark, 2011; Shaffer, 2017). These kind of behaviours where not even thought of as being addictive behaviours, considering how normal certain activities may seem, like for instance shopping and sex addictions (Hartney, 2019b). It should also be noted that, everyone and anyone could become a victim of addiction (Henderson, 2000; Moss & Dyer, 2010).

Phases of the Addictive Career

Addiction does not just happen overnight, but rather is a process that takes time to develop (Moss & Dyer, 2010; Hartney, 2019a). It is supposedly being said that the best way to formulate and understand addiction is by utilizing a career approach; similarly, to the one adopted to criminal behaviour (Clark, 2006). Through this approach, addictive behaviours occur along points on a continuum; which is not necessarily always a linear process. This is because an individual who is at stage one of the career, does not automatically mean that the individual will also engage in stage four (Clark, 2011). An addictive career has four stages, these being; onset, escalation, commitment and desistance (Clark, 2006; Clark, 2011). These stages represent the beginning (i.e. onset) and the end (i.e. desistance) of the addictive career, as well as the career length in between (Clark, 2011).

Onset. While adolescents are transitioning into becoming independent, young adults they are at a crucial phase in which they like to experiment with new behaviours (Wolfe, Jaffe & Crooks, 2006; Qidwai, Ishaque, Shah, & Rahim, 2010). For instance, more often than not adolescents experience using drugs or alcohol consumption for the first time during this phase so as, to impress and fit in with their peers (Albert, Chein, & Steinberg, 2013). Such experimentation could potentially lead to the beginning of the adolescent's addictive career (NIDA, 2018). Nonetheless, it does not mean that every adolescent that consumes drugs or alcohol on an occasional basis, like during the weekends, ends up being a substance or alcohol addict (Clark, 2011). In fact, the American Academy of Child and Adolescent Psychiatry (AACAP) mentions how certain adolescents will just experiment and then stop, if not entirely at least limit their consumption to infrequent basis, without having any significant troubles (Leipholtz, n.d.). Additionally, Clark (2011), continues to elaborate that "use may remain experimental ... and the individual may fail to progress along the continuum" (p. 61). Thus, will not lead an addictive career.

However, there are a few adolescents that end up developing an addiction, especially if they have been experimenting with such behaviours from a very early stage in their life (Leipholtz, n.d.). When young people whom are relatively still young in age develop an addictive career, it is referred to as early-onset. According to The European School Survey Project on Alcohol and other Drugs (ESPAD, 2015), results showed that the highest type of early-onset behaviours are that of; alcohol consumption (47%) and cigarettes (23%), amongst the students that took part aged thirteen or younger.

Escalation. Following the phase of onset, is escalation. During this stage addiction increasingly progresses to a point where the behaviour or substance dependence becomes very hard to control, excessive and prodigious (Coombs, 2004; Ahmed, 2011). The individual's mind and body is still not entirely hooked to the addiction, however continuous use of the substance or behaviour will lead to that path (Leipholtz, n.d.). At this stage, adolescents start acknowledging the negative repercussions that such addictions can have on their life like for instance, excessive consumption of alcohol leads to reckless driving and thus could potentially end up having their license suspended (Moss & Dyer, 2010; Clark et al., 2018). In cases where this happens, adolescents can deviate from repeating that particular behaviour. Besides that, such behaviours can also have positive effects on adolescents' life like for instance, decreasing stress or pain (Leipholtz, n.d.; McMurran, 1994; Taughinbaugh, 2013). If that's the case, adolescents are more likely to keep using or administering such behaviours, leading them to the next stage in the criminal career.

Commitment. Next comes the phase of commitment. This is the stage where addiction becomes totally uncontrollable up to a point where individuals cannot even manage to control their lives and behaviours anymore (Clark, 2011; Leipholtz, n.d.). The addicted person might start to believe that without the substance or addictive behaviour, he/she is not able to function properly or, that such addictions are a part of who they are (Henderson, 2000; Moss & Dyer, 2010; West & Brown, 2013). Also, individuals become rather preoccupied with the addiction throughout this phase, in the sense that, they start spending significant time engaging with such activities or behaviours up to a point where they even start neglecting both others around them and their routine activities, like going to work and school (Freimuth, 2008; Clark, 2011; Sussman, 2017).

Desistance. Lastly, comes the end of the addictive career. In this final phase, individuals try to potentially give up their addiction, or at least limit the activities or behaviours to a more controllable level (Frisher & Beckett, 2006; Weaver, 2019). At this point, individuals seek the necessary help from professionals as it is rather impossible for the individual to stop the addiction alone, thus requiring professional guidance (Clark, 2011; Leipholtz, n.d.). If adolescents attempt to immediately stop consuming alcohol, for example, they could end up with serious withdrawal symptoms or worse, even end up dead (Maisto, Connors, & Dearing, 2007). Hence, it is crucial that they take it seriously and seek the professional help they require.

The Four Models of Addiction and Potential Interventions

The four models of addiction have a crucial role in the addictive career. Each model represents the likelihood for an individual to become an addict, in light of the respective aforementioned phases in the addictive career as well as, presents potential interventions that can be adopted.

Disease and Choice Model. First model is the Disease and Choice Model. In light of this model, addiction is seen as being a chronic disorder that is caused by some sort of brain dysfunction, rather than being a temporary situationally activity or behaviour (Dunnington, 2011). This model portrays addict individuals as being the victims, who are blameless for their actions. Considering that they are 'sick', addicts are unable to think rationally about the choices they make (Schaler, 2000; Racine, Sattler, & Escande, 2017). Their choices of whether or not to engage in substance or addictive behaviours depends on the outcomes of such activities, for instance, if the pleasure outweighs the consequences than these individuals carry on with the activity, without thinking about any future repercussions the action might have (Heyman, 2009; Clark, 2011). Hence, their choice is completely voluntarily and they choose to engage in such behaviours daily out of their own free will. Furthermore, according to this model, addicts need medical treatment in order to be 'cured' from their disease (i.e. addiction) (Racine et al., 2017). A potential intervention could be raising awareness amongst adolescents about the fact that addiction is not a disease imposed on individuals, but rather individuals choose to engage themselves with addictive behaviours or activities. This way, adolescents became aware that they could opt-out from engaging in an addiction; since it is not a disease afflicted on them, they have a choice (Loverde, 2010)!

Biological Construct. Second model views addiction as a Biological Construct, in which addiction is seen as an inevitable biological source (Clark, 2011). There are two biological explanations which attempt to explain addiction, being; genetic characteristics and neuroadaptation (West, 2002). The former relates to the genetic disposition that individuals have. Several studies in the area, specifically twins, adoption and family studies, show that an individual's risk of becoming an addict is proportionate to the genetic relationship of an addicted relative (Bevilacqua & Goldman, 2009; Ducci & Goldman, 2012). Consequently, in light of this explanation, adolescents are unable to desist from the addictive career because of their inherited genes- it is their path (Goldberg, 2010; Lewis, 2015). The latter, relates to the changes that occur in the brain following the use of drug administration (West, 2002;

Seger, 2010; Mons & Beracochea, 2016). Example, adolescents that have previously engaged with alcohol consumption have developed drinking patterns in their brain. The next time they consume alcohol they would need to drink more than the last time in order to feel its effect, considering that they have increased their tolerance levels (ENA, 2013). Since the adolescents brain has adapted to alcohol use, they might experience feelings of longings, i.e. cravings, for alcohol thus leading them to future consumption (Waal & Morland, 1999). Failure to consume in the future will lead to withdrawal symptoms (West, 2002). Consequently, this model suggests that the addiction will only get worse as it keeps progressing; from onset to commitment, and then desistance (withdrawal). Lastly, such a model implies treatment as means of intervention; however, it also suggests that developing a neurodevelopmental perspective when implementing policies (especially focusing on vulnerable adolescents) might help in early intervention (Potenza, 2013).

Psychological Construct. Although closely associated with the above model, the psychological construct focuses more on the person-behaviour-environment interaction, rather than internalized processes alone (Clark, 2011). A set of theories in this area are the personality theories, amongst others; which focus on individuals as having an 'addictive personality', thus the reason why they are more prone to becoming addicts lies in their personality traits (West, 2002). Addictive personality individuals, specifically those who are; psychoticism, neuroticisms and extraversions, engage in addictive behaviours or activities regardless of knowing and understanding what the consequences are. For instance, studies show that since neuroticism personality type individuals suffer from emotional liability, like mood swings and extreme anxiety, they are more likely to engage in a substance related addiction, as it helps ease and control their feelings and moods (Sher, Trull, Bartholow, & Vieth, 1999; West, 2002). However, it is not concluded that personality traits alone lead to an addictive career as the environment has an important role as well (Clark, 2011). Learning theories allude that adolescents mimic the behaviours of those around them, especially their guardians. If, adolescents are exposed to an environment in which their parents have an addiction, they are more likely to become addicts themselves (Bates, 2019). That being so, according to this model, adolescents have no other choice but to lead an addictive career. A potential intervention could be encouraging treatment for those adolescents suffering from a personality disorder (such as OSD), like counselling sessions or therapy, so as to teach adolescents the appropriate ways of how to handle their feelings and mood swings without any form of substance-use and thus, hopefully avoid addiction.

Sociological Construct. The last model portrays the addictive career as being a sociological response; meaning that, addiction is acquired through both the interactions with other individuals in society, like close friends and family members, and also through the surrounding environment, like values and subcultural norms (Campbell, 2007; Clark, 2011; Hammersley, 2017). As mentioned earlier, adolescents are at a phase where they want to fit in with their peers, thus leading them to try out new behaviours, like for instance alcohol (Albert et al., 2013). When at clubs, or other places of entertainment, and their friends are consuming alcohol, adolescents are more likely to try it out themselves as socializing with their peers would require them to do so in order not to feel left out (Gilligan & Kypri, 2012; Carvajal & Lerma-Cabrera, 2015). Within the local context and society, it is not that difficult for adolescents to consume or buy alcohol, even if they are still under the legal age. In fact, finding alcohol is not that difficult as it is basically everywhere they go; even when buying local 'pastizzi' one can find alcohol! The Maltese society has a drinking average which is higher than the global average (Caruana, 2018). As a society, alcohol consumption is considered as being a normal behaviour, and does not require any special events or celebrations to be consumed. As a matter of fact, according to Caruana (2018), individuals in Malta drink approximately one to two alcoholic drinks per day; while a report by ESPAD (2007) showed that Malta ranked in third place, from the 35 participating countries, when a study was conducted regarding alcohol consumption in 15 to 16-year-old students. Living in Malta, makes it almost impossible not to drink and so, adolescents are exposed to alcohol from an early stage in their life (Pace, 2017). Thus, they are more at risk of leading an alcohol addiction. An intervention that can be introduced locally so as to potentially avoid alcohol addiction (specifically during the phase of early-onset) in adolescents, is trying to convince the state that by raising the prices of alcohol, the chances for adolescents to purchase it will decrease (Borg-Ellul, 2005). Considering that adolescents are not yet financially dependent, raising the prices of alcohol would make it harder for them to buy it as they would not afford it. Another intervention which could be useful during the escalation phase could be, raising more awareness about the fact that even tough alcohol is a legal drug, it is the most dangerous drug of all (Boseley, 2010; Lopez, 2015). Awareness could create a negative image and fear in the adolescents' mind, which could potentially deviate them from wanting to continue consuming alcohol (Caruana, 2019).

Conclusion

People use the word addiction all the time when talking, so it is important to differentiate between when a real addiction is occurring or not. This can be done by identifying the six core components of addiction, which according to Griffiths all need to be present in order for addiction to occur, these being; salience, mood modification, tolerance, withdrawal symptoms, conflict and relapse (2005; Kim & Hodgins, 2018). Even tough there is a good number of theories and models which attempt to explain the addictive career and addiction, they are all united. In fact, the four models of addiction presented above all interlink with each other, as their explanatory theories create a unified addiction phenomenon (Clark, 2019). Overall, addiction remains a construct which is still not completely understood as it is still being seen as a disease and thus, it cannot be entirely tackled (Lewis, 2016). That being so, I personally feel that more awareness regarding the construct needs to be raised in order to prevent future potential addicts, or at least, diminish the number of adolescent addicts.

References

Ahmed, S. H. (2011). Escalation of drug use. *Neuromethods, 53*, 267-292. Retrieved from

https://www.researchgate.net/publication/226195478_Escalation_of_Drug_Use

Albert, D., Chein, J., & Steinberg, L. (2013). Peer Influences on Adolescent Decision Making. *Current directions in psychological science, 22*(2), 114-120. doi: 10.1177/0963721412471347.

American Psychiatric Association. (2013). Substance-related and Addictive Disorders [PDF File]. Retrieved from

https://www.google.com/url?sa=t&rct=j&q=&esrc=s&source=web&cd=11&ved=2ahUKEwj20MPLwePiAhXBy6QKHRO3DCYQFjAKegQIARAC&url=https%3A%2F%2Fwww.psychiatry.org%2FFile%2520Library%2FPsychiatrists%2FPractice%2FDSM%2FAPA_DSM-5-Substance-Use-Disorder.pdf&usg=AOvVaw3Slip_zyF6pcuWerlspb9r

Bates, B. (2019). Cognitivism. In *Learning Theories simplified: And how to apply them to teaching* (2nd ed.) (pp. 43-58). London, UK: Sage.

Bedell, P. (2015). Recovery through the transformation to self-acceptance. In *What's your pain? What's your addiction?* (pp. 59-67). Retrieved from

https://books.google.com.mt/books?id=Uk-6CwAAQBAJ&pg=PA19&dq=what+is+addiction&hl=en&sa=X&ved=0ahUKEwiQ88_6nOLiAhVLzKQKHTOLDkE4ChDoAQg8MAQ#v=onepage&q=addiction&f=false

Bevilacqua, L., & Goldman, D. (2009). Genes and Addictions. *Clinical pharmacology and therapeutics, 85*(4), 359-361. doi: 10.1038/clpt.2009.6.

Borg-Ellul, D. A. (2005). *Risk perception, awareness and prevention measures to reduce underage drinking and the illegal purchase of alcohol in Malta.* Retrieved from https://books.google.com.mt/books?id=Cgfis3exRekC&pg=PA18&lpg=PA18&dq=raising+the+price+of+alcohol+in+malta+stops+adolescents+from+drinking&source=bl&ots=KS7U208mt7&sig=ACfU3U14AAY6OfYF1sysR_0PDzEJ38aB0Q&hl=en&sa=X&ved=2ahUKEwjI9fuq8eviAhXBs4sKHWGCDAwQ6AEwB3oECAkQAQ#v=onepage&q=raising%20the%20price%20of%20alcohol%20in%20malta%20stops%20adolescents%20from%20drinking&f=false

Boseley, S. (2010). Alcohol 'more harmful than heroin or crack'. *The Guardian.* Retrieved June 14, 2019 from https://www.theguardian.com/society/2010/nov/01/alcohol-more-harmful-than-heroin-crack

Campbell, N. D. (2007). Conclusion. In *Discovering Addiction: The science and politics of substance abuse research* (pp. 222-238). United States of America, USA: The University of Michigan Press.

Caruana, C. (2018, September 12). Adults have on to two alcoholic drinks a day. *Times of Malta.* Retrieved June 15, 2019 from https://timesofmalta.com/articles/view/maltese-drinking-higher-than-the-global-average.688942

Caruana, C. (2019, April 2). Police cannot be everywhere; minister says on drink0driving enforcement. *Times of Malta.* Retrieved June 15, 2019 from https://timesofmalta.com/articles/view/watch-police-cannot-be-everywhere-minister-says-on-drink-driving.706125

Carvajal, F., & Lerma-Cabrera, J. M. (2015). Alcohol consumption among adolescents-implications for public health. In D. Claborn (Ed.), *Topics in Public Health* (pp. 51-75).

Retrieved from

https://books.google.com.mt/books?id=WBCQDwAAQBAJ&pg=PA64&lpg=PA64&dq=adolescents+drink+in+order+not+to+feel+left+out&source=bl&ots=uC6QcLcjYn&sig=ACfU3U3Ynh-WHQmTsKo_uA5L-ON0_N9QBg&hl=en&sa=X&ved=2ahUKEwiqy8_16OviAhXIJVAKHdgQAHgQ6AEwCnoECAkQAQ#v=onepage&q=adolescents%20drink%20in%20order%20not%20to%20feel%20left%20out&f=false

Clark, D. B., Chung, T., Martin, C. S., Hasler, B. P., Fitzgerald, D. H., Luna, B., … Nagel, B. J. (2018). Adolescent executive dysfunction in daily life: Relationships to risks, brain structures and substance abuse. In, M. M. Torregrossa, J. M. Barker, & S. L. Gourley (Eds.), *Long-term consequences of adolescent drug use: Evidence from pre-clinical and clinical models* (pp. 9-22). Retrieved from

https://books.google.com.mt/books?id=ujhnDwAAQBAJ&printsec=frontcover&dq=negative+consequences+of+alcohol+on+adolescents&hl=en&sa=X&ved=0ahUKEwiO8N77hOTiAhUOU1AKHYzoA4YQ6AEIMTAC#v=onepage&q=negative%20consequences%20of%20alcohol%20on%20adolescents&f=false

Clark, M. (2006). Commitment to crime: The role of the Criminal Justice System. *European Journal of Criminology, 3*(2), 201-220. Retrieved frim

https://www.academia.edu/5957988/Commitment_to_Crime

Clark, M. (2011). Conceptualising addiction: How useful is the construct? *International Journal of humanities and Social Science, 1*(13), 55-64. Retrieved from

https://www.academia.edu/5957993/Conceptualising_Addiction

Clark, M. (2019). Addictive Behaviour [Powerpoint Presentation]. *Topic 1: Introduction.* Retrieved from https://www.um.edu.mt/vle/course/view.php?id=37203

Coombs, R. H (Ed.). (2004). *Handbook of addictive disorders: a practical guide to diagnosis and treatment.* Hoboken, New Jersey, NJ: John Wiley & Sons, Inc.

Diclemente, C. C. (2018). Understanding addictions in terms of change. In *Addiction and change: How addictions develop and addicted people* (2nd ed.) (pp. 3- 69). New York, NY: The Guilford Press.

Ducci, F., & Goldman, D. (2012). The genetic basis of addictive disorders. *The psychiatric clinics of North America, 35*(2), 495-519. doi: 10.1016/j.psc.2012.03.010.

Dunnington, K. (2011). Addiction and disease: Science, philosophy and theology. In *Addiction and virtue: Beyond the models of disease and choice* (pp. 15-30). Retrieved from https://books.google.com.mt/books?id=Ki4Rw_NIUeEC&printsec=frontcover&dq=addiction+and+the+disease+model&hl=en&sa=X&ved=0ahUKEwjDhI-mj-fiAhVRJ1AKHfRIATMQ6AEILDAB#v=onepage&q=addiction%20and%20the%20disease%20model&f=false

ENA. (2013). Basic clinical issues [E-Book]. In *Sheehy's Manual of Emergency Care* (7th ed.) (pp. 59- 182). Retrieved from https://books.google.com.mt/books?id=mAwCmKpnFs0C&pg=PA140&dq=tolerance+level+and+alcohol&hl=en&sa=X&ved=0ahUKEwj60_ednOziAhUPy6QKHULPDqcQ6AEINjAD#v=onepage&q=tolerance%20level%20and%20alcohol&f=false

ESPAD. (2007). The 2007 ESPAD Report: Substance use among students in 35 European countries. Retrieved from http://www.espad.org/sites/espad.org/files/The_2007_ESPAD_Report-FULL_091006.pdf

ESPAD. (2015). ESPAD Report 2015: Results from the European School Survey Project on Alcohol and Other Drugs. Retrieved from http://www.espad.org/sites/espad.org/files/ESPAD_report_2015.pdf?fbclid=IwAR1PvCHRO7jBQFTQzWPIStB4t6zn1shIKUw6A7rzIz2uViL_7Y_vFmnkfP4

Freimuth, M. (2008). *Addicted? Recognizing destructive behaviours before it's too late*. United States of America, USA: Rowman & Littlefield Publishers, Inc.

Frisher, M., & Beckett, H. (2006). Drug use desistance. *Criminology & Criminal Justice, 6*(1), 127-145. doi: 10.1177/1748895806060670.

Gilligan, C., & Kypri, K. (2012). Parent attitudes, family dynamics and adolescent drinking: Qualitative study of the Australian parenting guidelines for adolescent alcohol use. *BMC Public Health, 12,* 491. Retrieved from https://www.ncbi.nlm.nih.gov/pmc/articles/PMC3461436/

Goldberg, R. (2010). Motivations for drug use. In *Drugs across the spectrum* (6th ed.) (pp. 47-70). Belmont, Unites States of America, USA: Wadsworth Cengage Learning.

Griffiths, M. (2005). A 'components' model of addiction within a biopsychosocial framework. *Journal of Substance Use, 10*(4), 191-197. Retrieved from https://psycnet.apa.org/doi/10.1080/14659890500114359

Hammersley, R. (2017). How and why addiction is socially constructed. In, H. Pickard, & S. Ahmed (Eds.), *The Routledge Handbook of Philosophy and Science of Addiction* (pp. 1-18). doi: 10.13140/RG.2.2.17828.48008.

Hartney, E. (2019a, March 23). An overview of addiction and treatment [Blog Post]. *Very well mind.* Retrieved June 12, 2019 from https://www.verywellmind.com/addiction-4157312

Hartney, E. (2019b, May 26). An overview of behavioural addiction [Blog Post]. *Very well mind.* Retrieved June 11, 2019 from https://www.verywellmind.com/addictive-behaviors-4157291

Henderson, E. C. (2000). What is addiction? In *Understanding addiction* (pp. 1-11). United States of America, USA: University Press of Mississippi.

Heyman, G. M. (2009). Addiction and choice. In *Addiction: A disorder of choice* (pp. 115-141). United States of America, USA: President and Fellows of Harvard College.

Kim, H. S., & Hodgins, D. C. (2018). Component model of addiction treatment: A pragmatic transdiagnostic treatment model of behavioural and substance addictions. *Frontiers in Psychiatry, 9*(406). doi: 10.3389/fpsyt.2018.00406.

Leipholtz, B. (n.d.). The four stages of Addiction [Blog Post]. *Orlando Recovery Center: An advanced approach to patient care.* Retrieved June 8, 2019 from https://www.orlandorecovery.com/blog/stages-of-addiction/#gref

Lewis, M. (2015). *The biology of desire: Why addiction is not a disease.* Retrieved from https://www.amazon.com/Biology-Desire-Why-Addiction-Disease-ebook/dp/B00X2ZW9MM/ref=sr_1_1?keywords=9781925113914&linkCode=qs&qid=1560455777&s=books&sr=1-1

Lewis, M. (2016, June 7). Why it's wrong to call addiction a disease. *The Guardian.* Retrieved June 17, 2019 from https://www.theguardian.com/commentisfree/2016/jun/07/addiction-not-disease-science-stigma

Lopez, G. (2015). How scientist rank drugs from most to least dangerous- and why ranking are flawed. *Vox.* Retrieved June 15, 2019 from https://www.vox.com/2015/2/24/8094759/alcohol-marijuana

Loverde, M. (2010, June 16). The disease model and addiction [Blog Post]. Retrieved June 13, 2019 from https://family-intervention.com/blog/disease-model-addiction/

Maisto, S. A., Connors, G. J., Dearing, R. L. (2007). Diagnosis and treatment indications. In *Alcohol Use Disorders: Advances in Psychotherapy* (pp. 15-27). United States of America, USA: Hogrefe & Huber Publishers.

McMurran, M. (1994). Addiction: Misconduct and disease. In *The psychology of addiction* (pp. 1-28). London, UK: Taylor & Francis Ltd, Publishers.

Mons, N., & Beracochea, D. (2016). Behavioural neuroadaptation to alcohol: From glucocorticoids to histone acetylation. *Frontiers in Psychiatry, 7*, 165. Retrieved from https://www.ncbi.nlm.nih.gov/pmc/articles/PMC5052254/

Moss, A. C., & Dyer, K. R. (2010). What is addictive behaviour? In *Psychology of addictive behaviour* (pp. 1-18). Retrieved from https://books.google.com.mt/books?id=4bhgAQAAQBAJ&pg=PA17&dq=addictive+behaviour&hl=en&sa=X&ved=0ahUKEwip9Jq_vuHiAhUH16QKHZjPDF0Q6AEIOjAD#v=onepage&q=addictive%20behaviour&f=false

NIDA. (2018, July 20). Drugs, brains, and behaviour: The science of Addiction. Retrieved June 5, 2019 from https://www.drugabuse.gov/publications/drugs-brains-behavior-science-addiction/drug-misuse-addiction

Pace, Y. (2017, June 12). Keeping up bingeing tradition: Maltese teens tend to drink more than Europeans. *Malta Today.* Retrieved June 14, 2019 from https://www.maltatoday.com.mt/news/national/78062/keeping_up_bingeing_tradition_maltese_teens_tend_to_drink_more_than_europeans#.XQUbmi2B2b8

Pinna, F., Dell'Osso, B., Di Nicola, M., Janiri, L., Altamura, A. C., Carpiniello, B., & Hollander, E. (2015). Behavioural addictions and the transition from DSM-IV-TR to DSM-5. *Journal of Psychopathology, 21*, 380-389. Retrieved from http://www.jpsychopathol.it/wp-content/uploads/2015/12/12_Art_ORIGINALE_Pinna1.pdf

Potenza, M. N. (2013). Biological contributions to addictions in adolescents and adults: Prevention, treatment and policy implications. *The Journal of Adolescent Health: Official publication of the Society for Adolescent Medicine, 52*(2), S-22-S32. Retrieved from https://www.ncbi.nlm.nih.gov/pmc/articles/PMC3935152/

Potenza, M. N. (2014). Non-substance addictive behaviours in the context of DSM-5. *Addictive behaviours, 39*(1), 1-2. doi: 10.1016/j.addbeh.2013.09.004.

Qidwai, W., Ishaque, S., Shah, S., & Rahim, M. (2010). Adolescent Lifestyle and Behaviour: A survey from a developing country. *PloS one, 5*(9), e12914. doi: 10.1371/journal.pone.0012914.

Racine, E., Sattler, S., & Escande, A. (2017). Free will and the brain disease model of addiction: The not so seductive allure of neuroscience and its modest impact on the attribution of free will to people with an addiction. *Frontiers in Psychology, 8*, 1850. doi:10.3389/fpsyg.2017.01850.

Ross, D., & Kincaid, H. (2010). Introduction: What is addiction? In, D. Ross, H. Kincaid, D. Spurrett, & P. Collins (Eds.), *What is addiction?* (pp. vii- x). Retrieved from https://books.google.com.mt/books?id=iT2gVqGpB98C&printsec=frontcover&dq=what+is+addiction&hl=en&sa=X&ved=0ahUKEwjb6qv1keLiAhXJLVAKHdqIB8sQ6AEIJzAA#v=onepage&q=what%20is%20addiction&f=false

Ryan, F. (2014). Working with addictions. In, S. Llewelyn, & D. Murphy (Eds.), *What is clinical psychology?* (5th ed.) (pp. 153-168). United Kingdom, UK: Oxford University Press.

Schaler, J. A. (2000). Is addiction really a disease? In *Addiction is a choice* (pp. 11-20). Retrieved from https://www.amazon.com/Addiction-Choice-Ph-D-Jeffrey-Schaler/dp/081269404X/ref=sr_1_1?keywords=9780812694048&linkCode=qs&qid=1560452806&s=books&sr=1-1

Seger, D. (2010). Neuroadaptations and drugs of abuse. *Toxicology Letters, 196,* S15. Retrieved from https://doi.org/10.1016/j.toxlet.2010.03.080

Shaffer, H. J. (2017, June 19). What is addiction? [Blog Post]. *Harvard Health Publishing.* Retrieved June 10, 2019 from https://www.health.harvard.edu/blog/what-is-addiction-2017061911870

Sher, K. J., Trull, T. J., Bartholow, B. D., & Vieth, A. (1999). Personality and alcoholism. In, K. E. Leonard & H. T., Blame (Eds.), *Psychological theories of drinking and alcoholism* (2nd ed.) (pp. 54-105). New York, NY: The Guilford Press.

Sussman, S. (2017). Part I: Addiction and addictive effects. In *Substance and behavioural addictions: Concepts, causes, and cures* (pp. 1-85). United Kingdom, UK: Cambridge University Press.

Taughinbaugh, C. (2013, July 30). The four stages of drug use [Blog Post]. *Stop medicine abuse.* Retrieved June 12, 2018 from https://stopmedicineabuse.org/blog/details/the-four-stages-of-drug-use/?fbclid=IwAR0xDo-kughIsMScqWaUKrPa_roPnv0BfgubkRw6HlUau7UZMUvA07_hw60

Thombs, D. L., & Osborn, C. J. (2013). Conceptualization of addictive behaviour and the need for informed practice. In *Introduction to addictive behaviour* (4th ed.) (pp. 1-29). New York, NY: Guilford Press Publications, Inc.

Waal, H., & Morland, J. (1999). Addiction as impeded rationality. In, J. Elster (Ed.), *Addiction: Entries and exits.* (pp. 120-148). New York, NY: Russell Sage Foundation.

Weaver, B. (2019). Understanding desistance: A critical review of theories of desistance. *Psychology, Crime & Law, 6*, 641-658. Retrieved from https://www.tandfonline.com/doi/full/10.1080/1068316X.2018.1560444?scroll=top&needAccess=true

West, R. (2002). Theories of Addiction. *Addiction, 96*(1), 3-13. Retrieved fro https://doi.org/10.1046/j.1360-0443.2001.96131.x

West, R., & Brown, J. (2013). Definition, theory and observation. In *Theory of addiction* (2nd ed.) (pp. 10-36). Retrieved from https://books.google.com.mt/books?id=sWtwAAAAQBAJ&pg=PT42&dq=what+is+addiction&hl=en&sa=X&ved=0ahUKEwiQ88_6nOLiAhVLzKQKHTOLDkE4ChDoAQg1MAM#v=onepage&q=what%20is%20addiction&f=false

Wolfe, D. A., Jaffe, P. G., & Crooks, C. V. (2006). *Adolescent Risk Behaviours: Why teens experiment and strategies to keep them safe.* New Haven, London: Yale University Press.

YOUR KNOWLEDGE HAS VALUE

- We will publish your bachelor's and master's thesis, essays and papers

- Your own eBook and book - sold worldwide in all relevant shops

- Earn money with each sale

Upload your text at www.GRIN.com
and publish for free